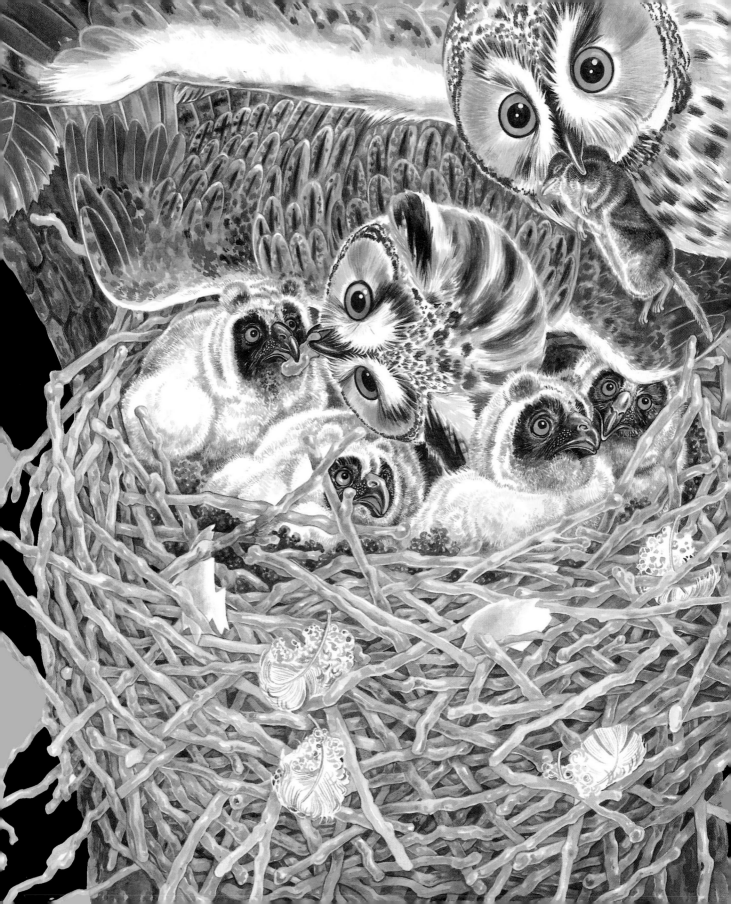

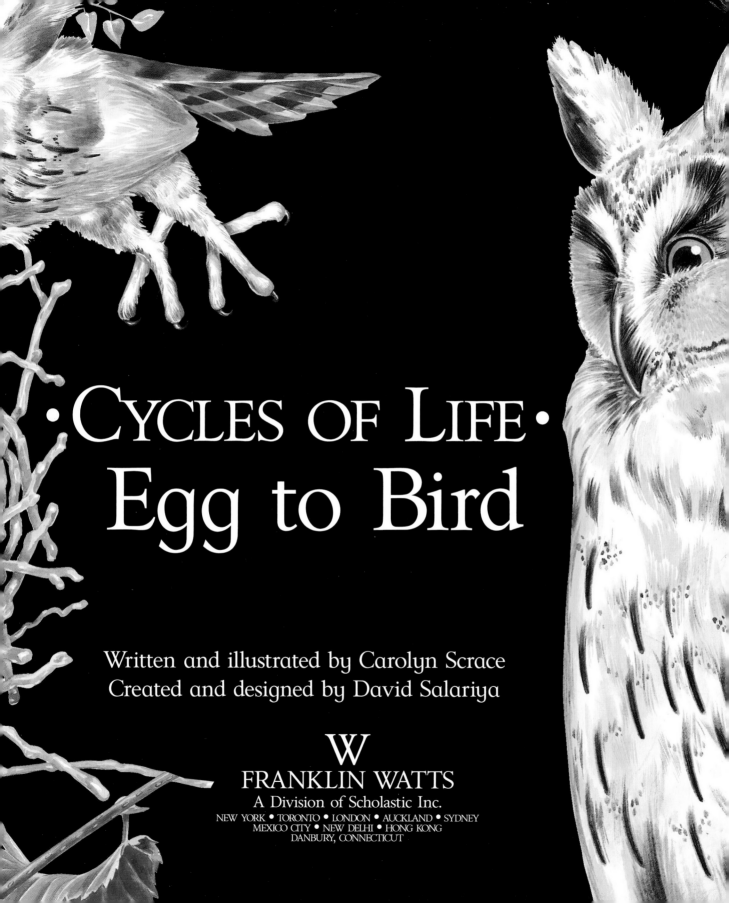

·CYCLES OF LIFE·
Egg to Bird

Written and illustrated by Carolyn Scrace
Created and designed by David Salariya

W
FRANKLIN WATTS
A Division of Scholastic Inc.
NEW YORK • TORONTO • LONDON • AUCKLAND • SYDNEY
MEXICO CITY • NEW DELHI • HONG KONG
DANBURY, CONNECTICUT

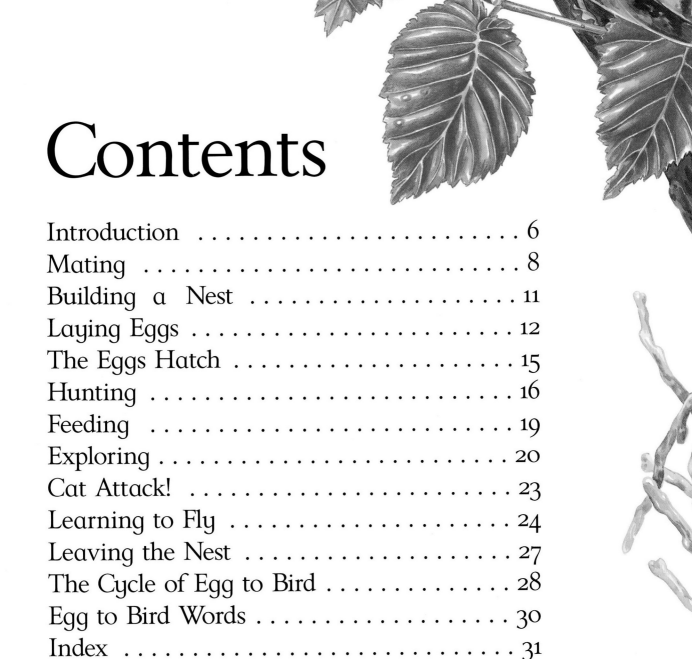

Contents

Introduction

Birds have two wings and are covered in **feathers**. Most birds, like the Long-eared owl, can fly.

A Long-eared owl begins its life inside an **egg**. When it has grown big enough, the baby owl breaks its way out of the **eggshell**.

In this book you can see the amazing cycle of life of a Long-eared owl, from egg to bird.

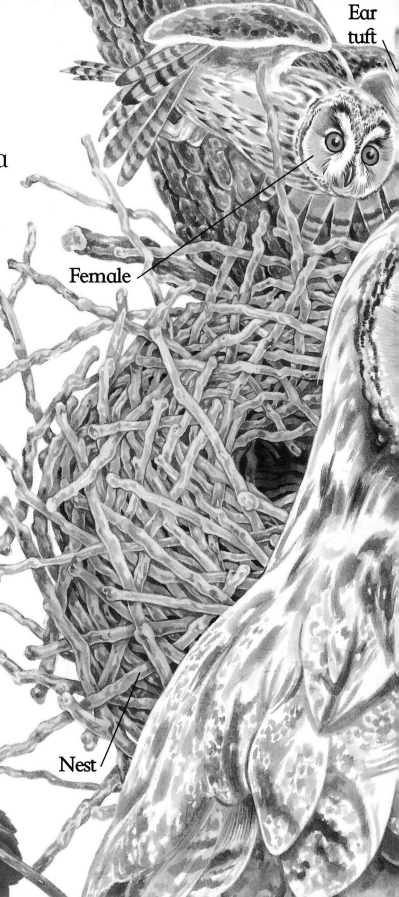

Mating

The male owl chooses a place to build a **nest**.

He then finds a female Long-eared owl by flying and calling in a special way.

When the female sees him she calls back.

The male and female owl then **mate**.

A Long-eared owl has large, orange eyes and long **ear tufts**. These are not its ears.

Ear tuft

Female

Butterfly

Nest

8

Male

9

Elm tree

Building a Nest

Long-eared owls
usually nest in the old
nests of other birds,
such as crows, magpies,
ravens, or herons.

The owls line their
nest with moss,
leaves, feathers, and
small pieces of bark.

The nest is high up in
the tree and is hidden
among the branches.

11

Laying Eggs

The female owl lays
from three to five eggs.
The eggs are white
and oval in shape.

The female sits on
her eggs to keep them
safe and warm.
Inside the eggs,
the tiny owls grow.

Sometimes the male owl
sits on the eggs while the
female hunts for food.

Egg

Caterpillar

12

13

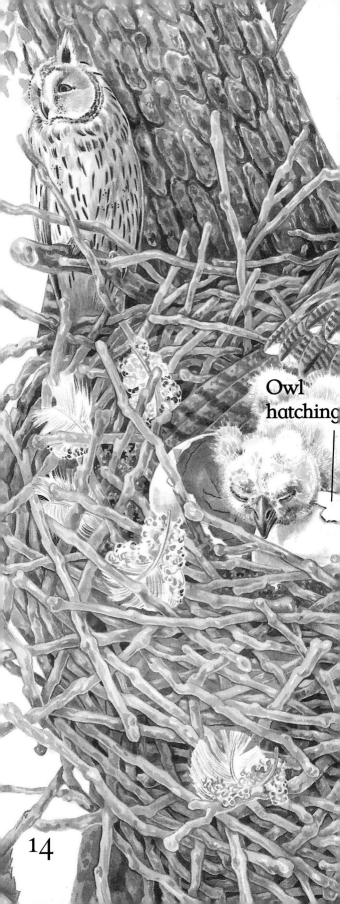

Owl
hatching

14

Nestling

The Eggs Hatch

After four weeks, the first egg starts to **hatch**. The tiny owl cracks open the eggshell.

When the baby owl comes out of the egg it is called a **nestling**. Nestlings are covered in fluffy, white feathers called **down**.

15

Hunting

At night, the male owl flies off and catches food for the nestlings.

The male owl takes food back to the nest. The female owl gives little bits to each baby.

Long-eared owls hunt at night and can find food even in total darkness.

Butterfly chrysalis

16

Feeding

Long-eared owls eat **mice**, rats, and other **rodents**. They also eat small rabbits and sometimes other birds or snakes.

The older nestlings make a call that sounds like a squeaky gate.

19

Exploring

Three weeks after hatching, the young owls can leave the nest.

They use their **beaks** and wings to climb and jump along the branches close to the nest.

Other birds and animals like to eat Long-eared owls. The adult owls keep watch over the young owls.

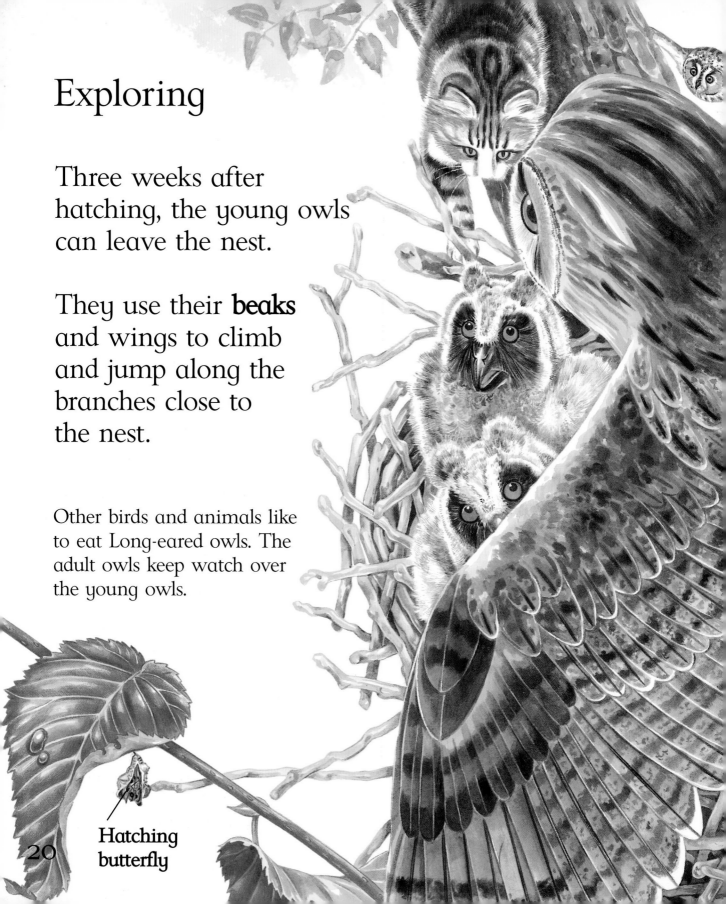

Hatching butterfly

20

Cat Attack!

When a cat comes near the nest, the female owl makes herself look as big and scary as she can.

She puffs out her feathers, spreads her wings out like a fan, and stares at the cat with her huge, orange eyes.

The adult owl makes a barking sound to frighten away the cat.

23

Learning to Fly

Five weeks after hatching the young owls begin to fly. At first they only fly a short distance.

They are always hungry and each night call for their parents to feed them.

A young owl is very curious. To help it see in every direction, the young owl can turn its head almost completely around in a circle!

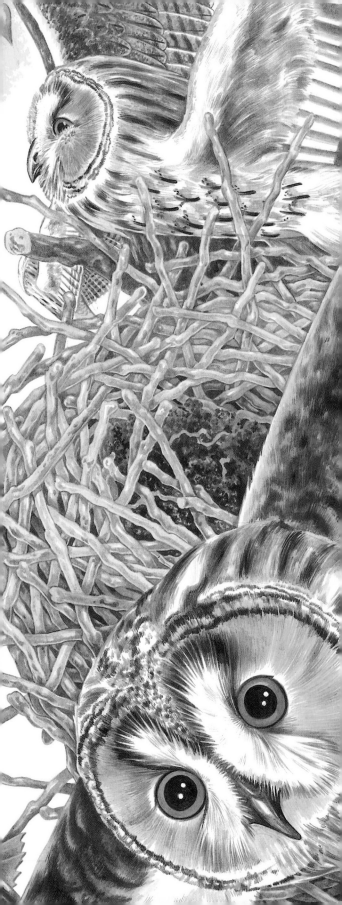

Leaving the Nest

Two months after hatching, the young owls can hunt for their own food.

It is time for them to fly away and leave the nest.

Long-eared owls usually live alone and only come together to mate and raise a family.

27

The Cycle of Egg to Bird

In spring, a pair of Long-eared owls build a nest. The female lays about three to five eggs.

About four weeks later, the eggs begin to hatch. The baby owls are called nestlings and are covered in white down.

During the next two weeks, the nestlings remain in the nest. They eat a lot and grow bigger and stronger.

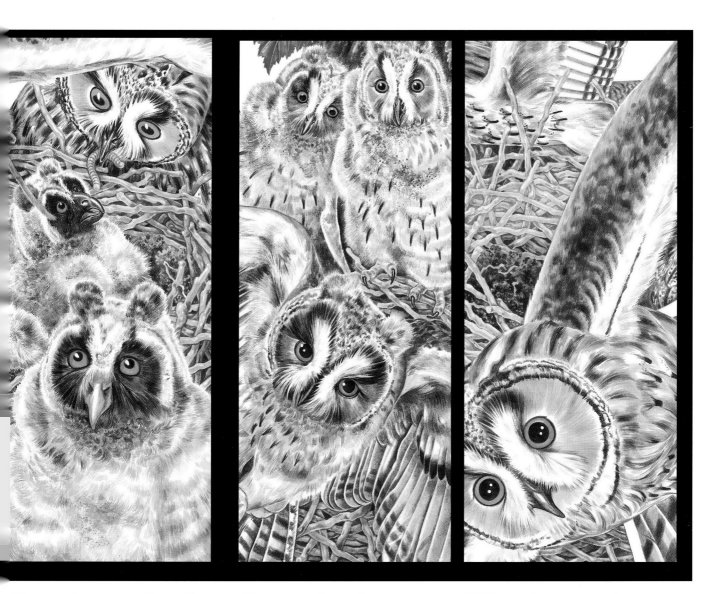

About three weeks after hatching the young owls are able to leave the nest and explore their surroundings.

Five weeks after hatching, they begin learning how to fly. Their parents still feed them.

When they are about two months old, the young owls leave the nest and hunt for their own food.

Egg to Bird Words

Beak
The hard and pointed area around the mouth of a bird.

Bird
An animal that has two wings and is covered in feathers. Most birds can fly.

Down
Soft, white, fluffy feathers that cover nestlings.

Ear tufts
Long feathery tufts on the top of the owl's head. These are not the owl's ears.

Egg
A container that holds the tiny, baby bird until it is ready to hatch.

Eggshell
The thin, hard covering of an egg. It keeps the baby bird safe as it grows.

Feathers
The light and soft covering of birds.

Hatching
When the baby bird leaves its egg.

Mating
When a male and female join together to have babies.

Mice
Small rodents.

Nest
A cup shaped bed made of sticks. It is used by a bird as a home for its young.

Nestling
A bird that is too young to leave the nest.

Rodent
An animal with two long, curved teeth which it uses for gnawing. Mice, rats, and squirrels are all rodents.

Index

Language Consultant:
Betty Root

Editors:
Karen Barker Smith
Stephanie Cole

Natural History Consultant:
Dr. Gerald Legg

Created, designed and produced by
The Salariya Book Company Ltd
Book House
25 Marlborough Place
Brighton BN1 1UB

Visit the Salariya Book Company at
www.salariya.com

A CIP catalog record for this title is available
from the Library of Congress.

ISBN 0-531-14661-8 (Lib. Bdg.)
ISBN 0-531-14840-8 (Pbk.)

Published in 2002 by Franklin Watts
A Division of Scholastic Inc.
90 Sherman Turnpike
Danbury, CT 06816

Printed in China.